THE STORYTELLING POCKETBOOK

By Roger E. Jones

Drawings by Phil Hailstone

"We live in the participation economy. A time when stories and conversations are what count; marketing has changed forever, moving from creating awareness and demand to inviting the audience to join a movement. And all movements are based on a great story. This book will help you become the best storyteller you can be. And it's fun too!"
Kevin Roberts, Worldwide CEO, Saatchi & Saatchi

"We don't always equate corporate CEOs with gifted storytellers, but rather as women and men who have learned the greatest number of facts and can share those facts with employees. What Roger Jones teaches us, however, is that 'great leaders are invariably your management skills, be a more y-to-day work', the Storytelling Pocketbook

the *New York Times* bestsellers, *MOJO*

Published by:
Management Pocketbooks Ltd
Laurel House, Station Approach, Alresford, Hants SO24 9JH, U.K.
Tel: +44 (0)1962 735573 Fax: +44 (0)1962 733637
Email: sales@pocketbook.co.uk
Website: www.pocketbook.co.uk

This edition published 2012 ISBN: 978 1 906610 40 1. Reprinted 2014

E-book ISBN: 978 1 908284 22 8

British Library Cataloguing-in-Publication Data – A catalogue record for this book is available from the British Library.

Design, typesetting and graphics by **efex ltd**.   Printed in U.K.

CONTENTS

Praise for the Storytelling Pocketbook

"I used to love stories as a child but never realised their power in business until I went to one of Roger's seminars. This book brings the power of the story to life in real and practical terms. It leaves the reader with a real sense of why stories matter, from the cooking (up a plot) stage, to the *when*, *how* and *where* of delivery. It's not just a must read for those engaged in engaging others, it's also an entertaining one."
Simon Levine, Global Practice Group Leader, DLA Piper UK LLP

"Good stories have impact. This helpful book gives you a practical guide on how to create, shape and deliver yours."
Rob Goffee, Professor of Organisational Behaviour, London Business School
and joint author of *Why Should Anyone Be Led by You?*

"The art of storytelling has become key to successful leadership and organisation change. Roger Jones' *how to* pocketbook gives today's managers the know-how to develop this art to make a real and practical difference to their leadership effectiveness."
Professor Frank Horwitz, Director, Cranfield School of Management

WHY STORIES MATTER

HOW THE AUTHOR DISCOVERED
THE POWER OF STORYTELLING IN BUSINESS

In November 1996 I worked for a multinational technology firm with responsibility for their key global customers. I had been asked to deliver our company's presentation at one of our industry's global conferences in Mexico. I prepared diligently: gathered lots of statistics and graphs, described product features and thought of ways to tell the audience why we were the best. I had a modest 50 PowerPoint slides.

In no time at all, there I was in the bland hotel conference room, walking up on stage to deliver my talk. The audience looked moderately interested. And I must confess I walked off the stage feeling a little smug, thinking I had done a pretty good job. I even received a warm ripple of applause.

My talk was followed by a coffee break, and I saw the next speaker, the CEO of a large US firm, getting ready to give his presentation. I must confess I thought: there's no way he's going to be as good as me.

HOW THE AUTHOR DISCOVERED
THE POWER OF STORYTELLING IN BUSINESS

He walked on stage but didn't stand at the podium as I had done, didn't use any prompt notes as I had done and didn't show any PowerPoint slides as I had done.

Standing at the front of the stage he told a whole series of stories, with just a few facts sprinkled in here and there. He told a change management story about how, as a wayward teenager, he had changed after talking to a policeman; when talking about sales growth, he didn't use graphs but talked about his blossoming garden; on leadership, rather than the usual examples of great generals and leaders from history, he talked about a teacher and the leadership lessons he learnt from her.

When he walked off stage, he didn't receive a warm ripple of applause as I had done – he got a standing ovation. My heart sank as I recognised what a poor job I had done, as a leader, in trying to inspire the audience with my logic. It was then that I realised that great leaders are invariably great storytellers.

It was then that I realised that storytelling solves the problem I had faced in the past – how to get your message to 'stick' and inspire people to take action. It was that experience that turned me into a storytelling advocate.

SO WHO IS THIS BOOK FOR?

This pocketbook is for anyone who wants to use pragmatic storytelling to help them achieve results in their day-to-day work. For example:

- Supervisors who want to have more productive team meetings
- Consultants who want to make the complex simple to understand
- Salespeople who want to engage customers on an emotional level
- Managers who want to increase their confidence levels
- HR professionals who want to engage employees
- Advertising executives who want to tell compelling stories for their clients
- Trainers who want their teaching messages to stick
- Executive coaches looking for a new tool
- Companies wanting to encourage innovation
- Company directors who want to get buy-in for their strategy
- Managers wanting to keep and harness the knowledge in their organisation
- Entrepreneurs wanting to excite people with their ideas
- Leaders who want to be more authentic and less remote…

And most importantly……YOU!

WHY WE NEED TO TELL STORIES

Everyday we are bombarded with information and our business world grows in complexity. At the same time we need a better way to persuade people, get our messages to stick and inspire action. PowerPoint presentations make audiences doze off, facts and figures are often dull and traditional change management techniques rarely convince.

We know anecdotally that stories are memorable, just from those we recall friends recounting. Yet few managers and leaders use storytelling as a strategic tool to communicate their organisations' values, get their people to embrace change and inspire even higher levels of performance.

Robin Dunbar, anthropologist and evolutionary psychologist, estimates that around two-thirds of our conversations are about who is doing what and with whom, ie stories. So storytelling is second nature to us all. Developing our innate storytelling skills helps us harness a natural activity – to tell stories – but in a purposeful authentic way with a clear business aim.

In this pocketbook we are going to explore how you can use storytelling in a pragmatic way to achieve results. So let's first look at some things stories can do, that facts, figures and logic can't.

WHERE STORIES BEAT FACTS

Stories are memorable. We are 20 times more likely to remember a fact if it is wrapped in a story.

Stories support how the mind works. Although we use left brain 'logical' thinking when, for example, we are solving problems, much of our thinking time comprises us telling ourselves 'mini' stories. Psychologists call this 'narrative thinking' – the stories we tell ourselves connect our thoughts, create tension and hopefully satisfy us.

Stories pull us towards the storyteller's conclusion. Think of a story as a bit like Aikido, a form of martial art that works by using another person's own momentum to propel him or her where you want. A story does the same. Whereas using facts is a push persuasion strategy, just like pushing a resistant donkey uphill.

WHERE STORIES BEAT FACTS

Stories convey emotions effectively and bring energy to our communication. We remember what we feel. And it's our emotions that inspire us to take action, **not** facts.

Stories spark our interest and have the ability to transport us imaginatively to places where we can visualise the events being recounted.

Stories help prevent what psychologists call 'confirmation bias'. It's the tendency for people to favour information that confirms their preconceptions, regardless of whether the information is true. As a result, people gather evidence and recall information from memory selectively, and interpret it in a biased way. So if someone tries to convince us to change our minds with facts and figures, we often dig our heels in and resist.

Confirmation bias occurs in change management initiatives, sales situations, when implementing strategies or making financial decisions, in politics and in our personal beliefs. But stories gently guide the listener, without proposing opposing facts, to **our** conclusions.

COMMON OBJECTIONS TO STORYTELLING

Now at this point you may be thinking, *'Hmm...I can see how these stories 'might' be useful, but is it really a good idea to tell stories in business? After all...'*

- *'No one else uses them.'* – Not true. You will see in the next chapter that companies around the world use stories to achieve business aims

- *'Stories are just 'fluff'!'* – They can be, but they don't have to be. We are going to focus on pragmatic storytelling

- *'I won't be able to find good stories.'* – It's much easier then you think to find good stories, as you will discover in the 'where to find stories' chapter

- *'Telling stories will make me appear to be an actor.'* – You may be a budding actor, but you certainly don't have to be. This book will show you how to tell stories in everyday business situations by being yourself

COMMON OBJECTIONS TO STORYTELLING

- *'Stories will make me appear boring.'* – Only if you repeat the same one over and over again. This pocketbook will show you how to develop and tell stories so you appear more authentic and confident

- *'Stories will never replace facts.'* – This is true in some situations, for example when it comes to sharing critical skills. You certainly wouldn't want a pilot to learn their job by listening to or reading stories. And there are times when only facts are appropriate, for example when you are presenting your financial results to shareholders

- *'Stories are not a panacea for all business problems.'* – This is true, but as you will discover when you read this book, stories can help you overcome your key business challenges

- *'Telling a good story is difficult.'* – Later in this book you will discover that storytelling is easier than learning to ride a bike

- *'The word 'story' will switch people off.'* – Yes that can happen, especially in professions based on logic like accountancy and engineering. In such cases, just use the term 'narrative' or 'narrative case study' instead

WHY STORIES MATTER

EXERCISE

Become a story detective:

- Listen to how your colleagues and customers use stories in their daily conversations

- Find out who in your organisation is a natural storyteller. Listen to how and when they tell stories. What can you learn from them?

- When you read a daily newspaper or watch the TV news, observe how journalists craft their stories

- Look at websites, charity mailings, promotional literature – stories are everywhere

Enjoy your storytelling journey and remember…

…you don't need an MBA to be a great storyteller.

WHO TELLS STORIES?

DEFINITION

I hope I have convinced you to use more stories. Let's now take a look at how various organisations have used storytelling to help them achieve their goals. Then we will embark on the practical detail of how you can find stories of your own.

But before continuing, let's briefly define a story.

Take a look on the internet and you will find a whole number of definitions. But there is no need to be too precise about something so natural. I like this loose definition:

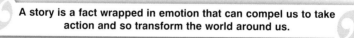

A story is a fact wrapped in emotion that can compel us to take action and so transform the world around us.

IBM & INNOCENT

IBM

Aligning everyone's actions to the company's strategy can be done effectively through storytelling. Lou Gerstner arrived as the new CEO in 1993. He didn't have a technology background and it was a time when IBM was a very troubled company. When it came to transforming the company and changing the culture for a group of people, Gerstner said:

'It is not something you do by writing memos. You've got to appeal to people's emotions. They've got to buy in with their hearts and bellies, not just their minds.'

And so he used powerful future stories about how the firm would transform into a services company. These stories were repeated and reinforced by his leadership team and spread around the company, gaining buy-in for the changes.

Innocent Drinks

Visit their website and you will see they have a story about how the founders gave up their jobs to start the business and how being accountable to their customers is something in their blood. There is also an engaging story of the highlights of their marketing journey. Their stories project the company as being fresh, customer-focused, innovative and personable.

CHARITIES, 3M & XEROX

Charities The power of keeping messages personal to engage potential donors is well understood by charities. They use powerful evocative images of humans in distressing situations. Annie Lennox, of *Eurythmics* fame, is a goodwill ambassador for UNAIDS. In an interview she gave to the Harvard Business Review, she was asked *'As an activist, how do you convey your message?'* Her answer: *'Human stories touch people, when you show them one child – not a statistic, a child.'*

3M Just take a look at 3M's website. You will see a section with the innovation stories they share with their clients to show they are leaders in their field, and stories they share internally to foster innovation.

Xerox They have a knowledge management system called Eureka. It gathers and shares tips/stories on service repair for technicians worldwide. The information captured in the system benefits other technicians who might face the same or a similar problem.

WHO TELLS STORIES?

CANON & RITZ CARLTON

Canon Fujio Mitarai, Canon's chairman, asks everyone to submit an annual business plan with a story. He writes a story about how the company can achieve the numerical goals he has established. That passes down through senior managers and middle managers to all employees. Everyone at Canon has to back up the numbers with a narrative. *'That's how skills are cultivated and our people grow,'* Mitarai explains, *'...it forms the foundation of Canon's strength.'*

Ritz Carlton The luxury hotel and resort group has over 30,000 employees around the world. Every workday every employee attends a team meeting. And at every team meeting they share real life stories of what employees have done at other hotels to exceed customer expectations. In sharing these tales, employees inspire not only one another but also themselves. I've attended one of these powerful storytelling sessions, and it's clear how this simple act of sharing a story about benefiting others can reinforce one's conviction about the purpose of a job. It's like creating a culture of mutual inspiration.

WHO TELLS STORIES?

GENERAL ELECTRIC, HITACHI & NIKE

General Electric In 1981 Jack Welch became CEO of GE. He felt the need to transform this successful company. Although its bureaucratic controlling structure had served it well in the previous 20 years, he realised it needed to be reinvigorated if the company were to adapt to the upcoming hi-tech environment. He succeeded in changing the organisation because of his ability to make the 'unknown land' acceptable to employees by using stories that were a commitment to the future.

Hitachi They ran an advertising campaign called *Hitachi True Stories*. It used emotional video storytelling in which customers spoke about how Hitachi made a difference in their lives. It employed documentary video techniques and social media. The campaign was well received for its originality.

Nike Its brand story challenges people to be empowered and 'just do it'. Its story inspires, continues to be popular and consistently hits an emotional chord with Nike's customers around the world.

LES SCHWAB, EUROPEAN WATERWAYS & US SCHOOL OF MUSIC

Les Schwab A tire-and-auto-repair chain in the Pacific Northwest, USA, has a strong reputation for going above and beyond in its customer service. Thousands of people have 'Les Schwab stories', in which they had a problem and a Schwab employee did something significant at no extra charge. They use these testimonial stories in their marketing as they are believable and help generate word-of-mouth marketing.

European Waterways A holiday company also uses storytelling in its marketing. Their interesting and compelling stories help engage their customers and are both a form of 'soft selling' to potential new customers and help bond past customers to them.

US School of Music Back in 1925 one of the most successful direct mail ads ever was written by John Caples for the US School of Music. Its headline has become legendary: *'They laughed when I sat down at the piano but when I started to play!'* His advert is an extended story about learning to play the piano. Caples rightly believed that storytelling has the power to enliven and drive action in copywriting. Since then storytelling has become the norm in direct mail.

WHO TELLS STORIES?

NASA & FEDEX

NASA As you can imagine, a space agency accumulates a vast amount of knowledge that needs to be passed on to future managers and leaders. It uses storytelling to communicate this wisdom. Take a look through their magazine entitled ASK to read some of these stories. (To find it just put the words 'Nasa Ask magazine' into your favourite internet search engine.)

FedEx They use powerful everyday work stories to great effect. One such story goes: In St Vincent, a tractor trailer accident blocked the main road going to the airport. Together, a FedEx driver and ramp agent tried every possible alternate route to the airport but were stymied by traffic jams. They eventually struck out on foot, shuttling every package the last mile to the airport for an on-time departure. The story demonstrates behaviours FedEx leaders want everyone in their company to exhibit. So instead of merely pleading for people to be persistent, innovative and collaborative, they shared this story as an example of what can be done (take a look at FedEx's YouTube video channel).

TYPES OF STORIES

ABOUT THIS CHAPTER

We've already seen why stories matter and how organisations use storytelling to achieve results. Shortly we will explore where you can find content for your stories, and then look at techniques to develop and tell them effectively.

But first it is useful to think about the types of stories we can employ in business.

As you read this chapter, bear in mind your current business challenges and think which type of story you might employ to overcome them.

WHO ARE YOU?

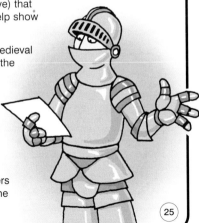

Revealing the life experiences (both positive and negative) that have shaped your values, beliefs and career path will help show people who you really are.

For many people their business suit acts like a suit of medieval armour that they hide behind, to prevent people seeing the real person. But the simple act of sharing an everyday event from your life can help your staff see the individual behind the job title.

Many clients I work with find that sharing a relevant personal story helps build their confidence. In addition, they often receive feedback that they appear more authentic.

Personal life stories are extremely important for managers and leaders. We will explore this type of story more in the next chapter.

THE FUTURE

It would be great if you could have your own crystal ball and see the future playing out in front of your eyes. Even better, think how useful it would be to show your staff and shareholders your crystal ball, allowing them, too, to see how the company navigates troubled times and enters this bright future picture.

Well, unfortunately, business isn't that simple.

As a manager and leader it is vital to tell stories that engage people's emotions as you paint the picture of your organisation's future vision.

Think how great orators from the past: Churchill, Martin Luther King, JF Kennedy, used powerful storytelling to inspire their audiences.

STRATEGIC

A company strategy that employees don't understand, don't believe in or simply can't remember is of no value.

The purpose of a strategy is to provide clear direction that helps everyone in your company perform their jobs in ways that contribute to achieving strategic goals.

Converting your strategic plan into a strategic story might just captivate not only the imagination of your executive team but also the hearts and minds of employees. Strategic stories explain the future picture, and evoke emotion and powerful imagery of what has happened in the past and what caused the turning point to adopt the new direction.

Remember, no strategy is truly unique, but putting it into a story might help you gain buy-in.

Call everyone to action at the end of your strategic story.

DEMONSTRATING VALUES

Many organisations' values are only formally communicated as lists of words that appear on corporate websites and in brochures.

Finding and using stories of employees demonstrating the desired set of values can help nurture and embed them within your organisation.

We looked at the example of Ritz Carlton in the previous chapter and how they use storytelling throughout their organisation to ensure their values are embedded with staff.

Thinking of your organisation, what are the top three values that are most important to it? Can you find three stories of staff demonstrating each value? How can you communicate these stories?

BRAND

Your brand is the stories people tell about your product or service. And stories help portray the human side of your brand and put customers at ease.

Marketers work hard to mould people's views of their product or services brand.

You are less likely to see advertisers describing a product's features; instead they will tell a powerful visual story that conveys the feeling (and often the attitude) of those who use their product.

Take a look at Harley-Davidson's advertisements on YouTube for great examples of brand storytelling.

The key is to use a narrative structure in your brand messages and choose the right story for your audience.

ENCOURAGING INNOVATION

Sharing stories of how others have successfully created new products or designed new processes can encourage others facing challenges to think more creatively.

Storytelling is also one of the most effective ways to demonstrate to your customers and employees how your new innovations can help them.

Although Dr Spencer Silver, a chemist at 3M, invented the adhesive that would be used on Post-it Notes in 1968, it wasn't until 1974 that his colleague Art Fry came up with the idea to use the adhesive to fasten notes in his hymnbook. Then six years later Post-its were launched. This story of innovation has gone on to inspire other scientists to discover new innovative products.

Many companies actively seek out these stories of innovation within their company and then harness them to encourage others.

MAKING THINGS HAPPEN

Being able to spark action effectively and make things happen is the desire of most managers and leaders.

In 1988 I worked for Chase Manhattan Bank. People would tell the story of how a particular executive would always pick up any litter that he saw, as he walked into the office building or as he walked around the office. The consequence of his action, and his simple story being retold, was that his floor of the office building was the tidiest I have ever seen. The lesson: your actions ignite stories and these stories influence the behaviours of others.

Telling a negative story to get people's attention and then following it with a positive future story with supporting rationale and a call to action, can help make it clear what needs to happen and encourage people to act.

MIND READING

There are times when it is useful to let others know that you know what they are thinking, as this can help deflate any resistance they are feeling towards your ideas.

Stories can prove a useful tool to do just this.

For example, you may know that a group of people are likely to object to your idea, because it has been tried before with limited success and they don't fully accept that changed circumstances mean that now it might work.

In this case you might tell a story about how another firm, in an unrelated sector but in similar circumstances to your own, had the same issue and successfully retried a very similar idea with great success. This story approach might reduce their resistance.

Good sales people are masters of this type of story as they try to melt away the objections of their prospective customers.

KNOWLEDGE MANAGEMENT

Knowledge management is, in part, about sharing 'lessons learned'. Storytelling is a proven way to pass on insights and experiences, since we are wired to be receptive to stories.

The sources of knowledge within an organisation are typically many and varied, and – as with all data we are exposed to – we suffer from information overload.

Storytelling, as part of a knowledge management strategy, has the power to cut through the noise. For this reason, storytelling may be the single most powerful enabler to share critical lessons within an organisation.

Storytelling helps prevent knowledge being lost when employees leave or projects come to their natural end. Importantly, storytelling plays a key role in how information travels, lessons are learned and knowledge is passed on to the new generation of managers.

SELLING

We all have to sell our ideas, whether or not we have the official title of sales person.

However, we have an inbuilt resistance to being 'sold to'. The hovering sales assistant in a shop may be better described as a 'sales prevention officer' in most cases. In business, professional buyers are always being sold to, and have 'closed their ears' to sales patter.

Oracle has adopted a 'storyselling' programme. This recognises that all of their technical knowledge, product training and problem-solving expertise are useless unless they can engage and interest the client.

A story can help bring your idea to life by conveying the emotional need it can satisfy. Top sales people tell compelling, credible stories that make the listener want to learn more.

WHERE TO FIND STORIES

INTRODUCTION

If you are going to follow the example of the companies described earlier and start to use storytelling for yourself, then the first step is to collect your own 'story library'. So let's look at how to find stories that you can use at work.

In essence, there are three main sources:

- Your personal stories
- Your organisation's stories
- Other people's stories

YOUR STORIES

Using your own personal stories has many benefits. For example, they can help you:

- Appear authentic
- Enhance your personal presence
- Develop your creativity
- Increase your confidence
- Be less remote by revealing a little about yourself

YOUR STORIES

You will hear motivational speakers telling their audiences how they overcame huge obstacles to achieve their goal of climbing a previously unconquered mountain, or rowing single-handed across a fierce ocean.

However, the most effective personal stories are about everyday experiences where you learnt something new. They don't need to be full of dramatic incident.

But how do you find your personal stories?

WHERE TO FIND STORIES

YOUR STORIES

Jot down the thoughts inspired by these questions. At this stage just note down the key points; we will look at developing them into full-blown stories in the next chapter.

- Some say the first seven years of someone's life are the most crucial and will determine what sort of adult they will be. What happened in your first seven years to shape you?
- Think of three specific times in your life when someone (perhaps a parent, teacher, coach or mentor) has had a positive impact on you
- Have you ever failed a job interview or lost your job?
- What are your three top character traits? Give an example when you have exhibited each?
- What have been the three major turning points in your life?
- What made you decide on your current career direction and why?

What other questions can you ask yourself to spark your thinking?

YOUR STORIES

Now take your list of experiences and note down next to each one:

- What, if anything, you learned from it
- What emotion(s) it produced in you at the time
- What emotion(s) it creates now when you think about it
- Who were the other major characters involved
- Whether you would you be happy to tell other people about it

You will discover how to develop these experiences into well-formed stories in the next chapter.

YOUR ORGANISATION'S STORIES

Let's now take a look at the next source – your organisation. Stories are the life blood and health barometer of all organisations. Managers and leaders who know the stories that are being told by employees and customers have their finger on their organisation's pulse. The first step is to become aware of the stories currently being told in your organisation.

- Do your technical staff read their manuals or do they swap stories in the canteen about their experiences repairing products?

- Your staff survey may give you a percentage score of your staff morale, but how do you capture individual experiences and stories that give true insights into what staff think?

- Your sales teams should have stories of how your customers use your products and/or services (these can be used in marketing campaigns)

- What stories get told to new recruits about your organisation and your leaders?

These narrative experiences are rarely effectively captured and too infrequently shared. But organisations that seek out this narrative experience develop a knowledge base that can be shared with all stakeholders to give them a greater sense of purpose.

YOUR ORGANISATION'S STORIES

For each story, you need to consciously decide what role you want it to serve, so you can collect the right material. If you would like it to be about, for example:

The value of your service	Gather stories from customers describing what it was like to interact with you and what they were able to do differently as a result.
Your foundations	Who started your organisation and why? Who inspired them?
Recruitment	Why did employees join your business? What inspired them?
Values	What are your firm's key values and what has happened in your business that demonstrates each value?
Nurturing values	Describe an experience when working in your company has meant something to you. Think of a time when your firm did something you admired.
Company future	Describe the future as a story that has already happened.

You can achieve a great return on your investment from organisational stories, as you will discover in the chapter on where to use stories.

OTHER PEOPLE'S STORIES

Other people's stories can be found literally everywhere.

Look for stories from history books, business books, business blogs, your neighbours and friends, daily newspapers and TV news, films and documentaries, psychology books, biographies and obituaries.

OTHER PEOPLE'S STORIES

There are several benefits to be gained from using other people's stories:

- It keeps things fresh – using a recent story from the press can help keep your message topical

- You can explore other worlds – taking your audience to an unfamiliar place can further add to their sense of intrigue

- You avoid the I.W.W.B.W.T.T.B. syndrome – if you use a story from an unfamiliar world, (though it must be one your audience can still relate to), you will stop them thinking '*it won't work because we've tried that before*', because the chances are it hasn't been tried in your workplace before

SOME WORDS OF CAUTION

As you start to collect your stories from all your different sources, you need to judge whether your audience will connect with your story. It might be wise to avoid:

- Sports stories – these can have limited appeal unless you are telling them to the team's fans (Exception – you have just won a gold medal at the Olympics against the odds!)

- Political stories – unless you are talking at your favourite party's annual conference

- Religious stories – these are best left to the pulpit

WHERE TO FIND STORIES

EXERCISE

Personal
List at least seven personal experiences that taught you something, or allowed you to see something or somebody in a new light.

Organisation
Thinking of your organisation, identify three of the current untold stories that might help you and your team in your endeavours.

Other person
Look for a good story about someone else that has a great message you could share.

Constantly be on the lookout for engaging new stories.

HOW TO DEVELOP A STORY

HOW TO DEVELOP A STORY

INTRODUCTION

By now, you have discovered some of the benefits of
storytelling, seen how other companies use stories,
have an idea of the types of stories you can employ,
and have started to collect some of your own.

The next step is to develop your stories further
so they are truly memorable.

In this chapter we will first look at some
story themes you can use and then
some ingredients that make everyday
stories stand-out.

HOW TO DEVELOP A STORY

STORY THEMES

1. CHALLENGE

All stories are built on variations of themes that have been around for thousands of years. Here are three of the most useful:

The classic challenge plot
Watch any great film and it is likely to derive its power from these basic characteristics:
- A main character (protagonist) the viewer cares about – we need to identify with them
- A catalyst compelling the protagonist to take action – the world has been turned upside down and the hero/heroine needs to put things right
- Trials & tribulations – obstacles occur causing set-backs and frustration. These can cause change in the protagonist
- A turning point – the protagonist realises he/she can no longer continue doing things the same way as before
- A resolution – the protagonist succeeds in his or her quest

The classic challenge theme is inspiring because it appeals to our perseverance and courage. Stories like this make us want to work harder and overcome challenges.

> **The challenge theme story can inspire people to take action**

HOW TO DEVELOP A STORY

STORY THEMES

2. CREATIVITY

With the **creativity theme**, the lead character in your story solves a difficult problem or shows innovative thinking or makes some type of breakthrough.

The basic structure of the story can be a simple adaptation of the classic challenge plot. A challenge is faced and a 'light bulb' moment occurs that enables a vital new idea to come to the fore. Many products we take for granted today were discovered in this way, for example, the Post-it Note (put the words 'post-it note story' into your favourite search engine to find out more).

The protagonist can be an individual or a team. The challenge can be anything from how to cut production line delays, to changing an organisation's structure, to raising funds for a new venture.

> **Creativity themes help spark innovation and encourage
> listeners to think differently**

STORY THEMES

3. CONNECTING

Connecting themes are ideal if you want to foster better teamworking relationships within your organisation or with your customers. These stories are about groups of people that build bridges to those with opposite opinions, backgrounds or opposing goals.

The plot is simple. A person going about their everyday life has something happen to them that connects them to someone who is a polar opposite. The story of the Good Samaritan is a good example; another is the film *Titanic*, where upper-class passenger Rose meets drifter and artist (and third-class passenger) Jack Dawson.

The connection themed story doesn't have to have 'life-or-death' consequences.

> **Connecting themes can help us appreciate opposing views, be more tolerant and understand other people's worlds**

ESSENTIAL INGREDIENTS OF GREAT STORIES

We've looked at three classic story themes – challenge, creativity and connecting. Now we need some extra ingredients you can add to your stories to make them work even better for you.

Human element: We are interested in people not data. People like to hear stories about people. A human element will help engage and bond listeners to your story. Build a central character into your stories – it might be you!

Unexpectedness: From young children to the leaders of global companies, we all like to be surprised, one reason why action movies are so popular. A good story creates questions in the mind of the listeners that they want to have answered. Introducing an element of surprise is a good way to achieve this.

ESSENTIAL INGREDIENTS OF GREAT STORIES

Detail: Give enough detail for listeners to paint a mental picture but not so much that you describe every colour and object. Allow them to visualise their picture, not your picture. If I say '*A frosty winter's morning in the countryside*', that is all you need to hear – you will immediately conjure up your own image.

Credibility: Stories are more about being plausible than accurate. The credibility comes from who is telling the story, the characters in it, its authenticity and appropriateness for the message you are delivering.

Emotion: We remember what we feel. Stories with no emotion are bland. Create emotional tension in your story and you will keep your listeners spellbound. If a 'big grizzly bear' jumps out in your story, state how you felt.

Journey: Stories are about pictures, not words. Your job as a storyteller is to transport your listeners to another place and time so they can relive the experience with you. Take them on a journey to entice them into your stories.

ESSENTIAL INGREDIENTS OF GREAT STORIES

... and they all lived happily ever after!

Message: Your story needs to make a point, a message that your listeners can take away and think about or act upon. Think about the learning point you want to convey. Don't, however, use a story's message to preach or even rant about your pet topic.

Brevity: A great story could be just 30 seconds long or it could be 30 minutes, or even an hour. But in general, keep your stories to two or three minutes in length. Less can often be more.

Positive ending: A story can take listeners on a roller-coaster of emotions but aim to finish on an uplifting note rather than have your hero toppling off a cliff. There is a lot to be said for *'happy ever after'* when you want to engage and inspire people.

HOW TO DEVELOP A STORY

ESSENTIAL INGREDIENTS OF GREAT STORIES

Focus: Think of your story as a straight railway line going from point A to point B. It should have a clear direction. As soon as you start to take your listeners into sidings and detours on your railway line (as interesting as they may be to you) you risk losing them and diluting the meaning of your story. Don't meander.

Resonance: Surprisingly simple stories can be powerful when they resonate with the listener. Stories that are familiar and stress commonality are more likely to resonate.

Contrast: Emphasising contrast in your story can help create interest and energy. If you travel between the contrasting views, your audience will be drawn further into your story. Think of the contrasts you can build in, for example: *'what would happen if the company changed?'* versus *'what will happen if it doesn't change?'*.

ESSENTIAL INGREDIENTS OF GREAT STORIES

Let's quickly recap –
does your story:

Have a human element?
Create an unexpected moment?
Allow the listener to fill in the detail?
Have credibility?
Express how you felt?
Take the listener on a journey?
Deliver a message?
Keep to the right length?
Have a happy ending?
Keep right on track?
Resonate with people?
Have an element of contrast?

HOW TO DEVELOP A STORY

STORYBOARDING

Storyboarding your story can help you see how it will flow. Here is how to do it:

Take a piece of paper and draw, say, eight equal squares. Now think of your story as scenes from a film: what will be happening in each scene as your story builds? Is there anything you can do to make each scene more vivid and appealing?

Once you have put your story into your storyboard check it has the story ingredients we just read about.

Now produce two versions of your story – one around three minutes in length and the other just 30 seconds long – it can be done!

You may just have developed the foundation of the next Hollywood blockbuster script.

STORYBOARDING

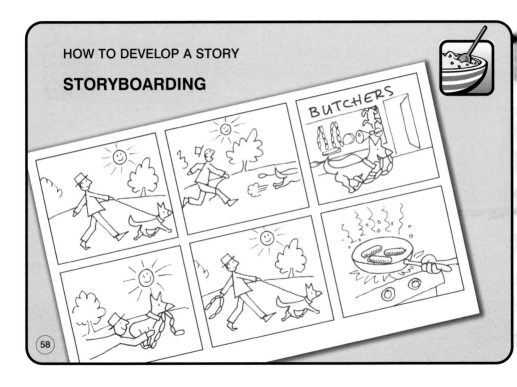

YOUR STORY LIBRARY

I suggest you develop a library of your favourite stories, using the guidelines shared in this chapter.

You don't need to write them out word for word, just create a skeleton outline or storyboard, whichever you prefer, for each one. Put them in a notebook or add them to your computer folders.

Add one new story each day for a month and your library will rapidly grow.

HOW TO DEVELOP A STORY

YOUR STORY LIBRARY

As your story library grows, make a point of reviewing each story and ask yourself:

- What type of audience will it appeal to?

- What type of hard data will this story support?

- Do I believe in this story 100%?

- How long will it take to tell?

- What will my audience think about me as a result of experiencing the story?

HOW TO DEVELOP A STORY

EXERCISE

Find a magazine article that's story based.

What theme does it follow?

- Does it have a human element?
- Does something unexpected occur?
- What level of detail does it contain?
- Is it credible?
- Does it display emotion?
- Where are you transported?
- What's the meaning of the story?
- Does it resonate and have contrast?

How could you improve this story if you were to rewrite it or recount it to an audience?

HOW TO DEVELOP A STORY

RECAP

Before moving on, let's quickly review what we have explored so far:

- We started by looking at why stories matter. Did I convince you?

- We went on to look at examples of how businesses around the world use storytelling to accomplish their goals. Which of these examples resonated with you most?

- Then we identified the main types of stories we can use in business. Which may be of most value for you?

- From here we explored the three main areas where you can find stories: your personal stories, your organisation's and other people's. What story ideas have come to mind so far?

- Most recently we looked at how to develop a story so that it engages your audience

Now we are going to look at how to **tell** your story.

How to tell your stories

INTRODUCTION

Congratulations! By now you have developed some stories and you are ready to deliver one in front of a live audience, perhaps at a meeting, presentation or team away-day.

Of course, not all storytelling has to be delivered face-to-face, nor rely primarily on words to convey its key message. In this chapter we review the different media and forms available to you. Then we will look specifically at oral storytelling and some techniques and tips that will help ensure you deliver your stories confidently, so that your audience enjoys your performance.

WHAT STORYTELLING MEDIUM TO USE

A few hundred years ago when only a select few could read and write, oral storytelling was the only means open to most people. But today we have many choices. Let's take a look at the various media available to tell our stories, and some pros and cons of each:

A photograph – with a brief caption can be extremely powerful. Before and after photos are the staple of many cosmetics adverts, as they tell the story of how the product can benefit their would-be customers.

Notice how charities use deceptively simple photos to transmit their emotionally laden stories. Take a look at almost any charity website for examples of their photo stories.

Look closer!

WHAT STORYTELLING MEDIUM TO USE

Video – record a video on your mobile or camcorder of your customers' stories about how they use your products and/or services. If you have a bigger budget, a short documentary of how employees have gone the extra mile might spur others to do the same. Put the videos on your blog, website, or on YouTube for the whole world to see. Take a look a FedEx's YouTube channel for examples of how they do just this.

Written prose – I am not suggesting you sprinkle stories in the margin of your next budget spreadsheet but there are places where a written story can work well. For example, customer stories on websites can be more engaging than case studies, or you could follow Canon's example (see page 19) and add a story to your annual business plan.

Asking employees to share their stories on your intranet might help further engage them, or you could start a database of stories just like Xerox (see page 18).

ORAL STORIES

Your main use of stories, however, is likely to be traditional oral delivery to a group of people. In the following pages we look at how to:

- Remember your story
- Use your voice and spice up your words
- Think from your audience's perspective and boost your confidence
- Start your story and be a story listener
- Use a neat advanced technique
- Collect your signature stories

REMEMBERING YOUR STORY

First, you need to embed your story in your mind, so you are confident and fluent when telling it. Experiment with different techniques to see what works best for you. Possibilities include:

- Writing it out a few times
- Thinking of it as scenes from a film
- Creating a mind map
- Recording and listening to it

HOW TO TELL YOUR STORIES

YOUR VOICE

If you are using a story to help deliver a serious message, you will be best keeping to your normal business conversational voice. Or you could use the politician's trick of talking in a slightly deeper and slower voice, if this feels comfortable for you, as it may make you sound a little more authoritative.

In less formal situations you could bring more variety into your voice:
- A quieter voice can be as effective at getting listeners' attention as turning up the volume
- Vary the speed
- Use pauses
- Use slightly different voices to dramatise the roles of different players in your story (if appropriate)

If you are concerned that you are not using enough voice variety, imagine you are telling the story to a group of four year olds – if you don't use an entertaining voice they will soon get bored.

You will find your story's natural rhythm and tempo after you have told it a few times.

YOUR WORDS

Spice up your story by using rich everyday language. For example:

Visual words: reveal, focused, hazy, flash, twinkle, reveal, dawn, imagine, vivid.

Sensory words: grasp, feel, touch, suffer, stumble, tap into, slip through, relaxed, cool, in touch.

Auditory words: deaf, outspoken, echo, snap, hum, tune in, harmonise, attune, resonate.

Use words that will help pull your audience into your story and help them to visualise the journey.

HOW TO TELL YOUR STORIES

YOUR AUDIENCE'S NEEDS

This simple exercise, called 'second position', will help you better understand your audience's needs, before you deliver your story at a meeting, conference or training session.

First Position:
- Stand where you are going to tell your story or sit in the chair you will be using
- Imagine telling the story and observe your imaginary audience
- Think about what you feel, see and hear as you tell your story
- Then ask yourself, *'How could I change how I deliver the story to make the experience more effective?'*

Second Position:
- Now sit in at least one of the seats your audience will occupy. If you know their job title or background, imagine what point of view they are likely to take
- Imagine ɣou are them listening and watching you tell your story
- Ask yourself what you feel about the story and how it is being delivered
- Then ask yourself, *'How could I change how I deliver the story to make the experience more effective?'*

VISUALISATION

Standing and delivering your story may well make you feel jittery at first. If so, try this visualisation technique; it is a great confidence booster.

Now I want you to imagine yourself doing something that you can do really well. Something you are supremely confident about, eg riding a bike, cooking, playing a particular sport or a musical instrument, or maybe you are supremely confident that you are a good parent.

Whatever it is, picture the activity in your mind as if you are reliving the experience. Take note of the colours in your picture: are they bright or dim? Is the picture sharp or blurred? Is it three dimensional or flat? Now note where the picture is in the space around you: is it near or far? To the right or left, up or down? Now with your eyes still closed point to it. Remember exactly where the picture is.

HOW TO TELL YOUR STORIES

VISUALISATION

In a few moments, close your eyes again and imagine telling your story. When you do, change the brightness, focus and all the other visual characteristics to those you saw when you imagined doing the activity you are supremely confident about. Then think where the picture of you telling your story is in relation to the space around you. Wherever it is, I want you to move it to where you saw the picture of you acting confidently. Hold it there.

Repeat this exercise whenever you are about to deliver a speech. As if by magic, you will discover your confidence levels rocket.

PREPARING TO DELIVER YOUR STORY

It's show time! Here are some quick tips to help ensure you perform at your best.

Mental rehearsal – imagine what you will see, feel and hear as you deliver your story. Imagine the audience fully engaged with your story and congratulating you after you have recounted it. Make it so real that you could be watching a recording of your best ever performance. Play this recording in your mind frequently in the days leading up to your storytelling event.

A quiet space – find a place where you can relax and get fully engaged with your story before you walk out on stage or into your meeting. Think how you felt when you first experienced the events in the story, or how those in the story might have experienced them, if it isn't about you.

PREPARING TO DELIVER YOUR STORY

Relive the experience – when you are telling your story, relive the experience in your mind, as if you were in that situation at that moment.

Be present – stay fully engaged with the story as you tell it. Don't let your mind wander (especially if it is a tale you have told a few times before).

Timing is key – keep a clock in sight, and if you are over-running cut to the end as soon as practical.

Eye contact – make your audience part of your story. Watch how a skilled storyteller draws the audience into the 'telling' through eye contact.

Be flexible – Remember, accuracy is not the key. If you forget part of your story no one will know except you.

HOW TO BEGIN

Starting your story correctly is vital if you are to capture the audience's attention. You could begin with:

- A five second pause – this will get everybody's attention as you make eye contact with your audience
- A place – *'When I was in Mexico…'*
- A time – *'In November 2005 I was…'*
- A statement to gain attention: for example, I start one of my stories with the following statement: *'If you aim for the moon, you will hit the ceiling. If you aim for the ceiling, you will fall flat on your face.'* I pause and then begin my tale
- Segue into your story with: *'That reminds me of…'*

HOW NOT TO BEGIN

Never start by saying:

- *'I'm going to tell you a story…'*, because it might conjure up thoughts of children's books

- *'I'm going to tell you a **true** story about…'*, as your audience might think you don't normally tell the truth

HOW TO TELL YOUR STORIES

STORY LISTENING

Listening to the ways in which others tell stories will help you appreciate what it is like to be in the audience, what works and what doesn't.

- Actively listen when others recount their stories

- Ask yourself what you feel they do particularly well, what they might have missed out

- What could they do even better next time?

AN ADVANCED TECHNIQUE

This technique is sometimes called 'nested loop'. It's highly effective for embedding your key message if you are delivering a presentation, seminar or workshop.

A 'nested loop' is when, at the very start of your speech or workshop, you begin to tell your story and then stop just as you reach your obstacle or crisis point. You then leave the story and deliver all the content of your speech or workshop. At the end you pick up where you left off, ie say how you overcame your obstacle and complete your story.

Start your story and stop just when you reach your challenge or obstacle.

Now deliver your presentation.

Now go back to your story exactly where you left it, overcome your obstacle and resolve your story. Its message will reinforce the main message of your presentation.

79

AN ADVANCED TECHNIQUE

Let me give you an example: I often give a conference speech that carries the message that small changes will help you succeed.

I start by telling the story of how I ran the New York marathon. I stop the story just at the point when I hit my obstacle – in this case when I hit what runners call 'the wall' at mile 21 and couldn't move. I faced certain failure, or at least so I thought.

I then deliver the entire content of my presentation.

At the end of my speech I finish my New York marathon story. I say how I overcame my obstacle and actually completed the marathon by making 'small changes' to my running style. I then reflect the 'small changes to your style' message back to the audience by saying something along the lines of: *'just by making a small change in your communication style you too can reach your goal'*.

SIGNATURE STORIES

After you have recounted all the stories in your library several times, you will find some of them work particularly well.

Aim to develop these into your 'signature' stories.

These are the stories that you find most effective at getting your messages across.

Always look for ways to further improve your 'signature' stories.

HOW TO TELL YOUR STORIES

EXERCISE

If you are new to storytelling in business, then start recounting stories in front of safer audiences, perhaps at your team meeting. Then, as your confidence grows, experiment by spicing up your important presentations with stories.

Ask for feedback on your storytelling from someone you respect.

Listen to great storytellers you admire, perhaps in your organisation or in the outside world. What can you learn from them that you can integrate into your own storytelling?

WHERE TO USE STORIES

INTRODUCTION

In 1992 I moved to Madrid, Spain. I conscientiously attended all my Spanish language classes and diligently completed all my homework, **but** for a couple of years I failed to put my new knowledge about how to speak Spanish into action, in day-to-day situations such as talking to taxi drivers and in bars and shops. The consequence was that I learnt and knew everything about Spanish grammar and could read the daily newspaper, but I made slow progress with my Spanish speaking skills until I simply plucked up courage to use them regularly in everyday situations.

I eventually became a good Spanish speaker, but five years later, when I moved back to London, I stopped using Spanish and my language skills have now become very rusty.

The same applies to storytelling.

To become confident storytellers, we need to use our storytelling skills whenever appropriate in day-to-day business.

Let's take a look at some of the everyday business situations where storytelling can be used to good effect.

PRESENTATIONS & MEETINGS

If you think of a great presenter you have seen, the chances are that he or she used at least one powerful story to bring the message to life.

Take a look through some of the standard presentations you deliver within your company, or to clients and other stakeholders. Is there a story or two you could use that will reinforce what you are trying to get across and make your presentation more memorable? If there is, use it at the beginning of your presentation to captivate your audience.

Meetings
Alan Kay, a Hewlett Packard executive, is quoted as saying: *'Scratch the surface of a typical boardroom and we're all just cavemen with briefcases, hungry for a wise person to tell us stories'*.

Could you be the wise person and start to purposefully use pragmatic storytelling in the meetings you attend?

WRITTEN MATERIALS & SURVEYS

From blogs to company annual reports, from proposals to your resumé and from direct mailing letters to your strategic plan, a story might help set you apart from the crowd.

Keep it brief and make sure it resonates with your message. Your stories can help humanise what might otherwise be a cold business communication.

Surveys
Asking respondents to give examples (or mini stories) when they answer an employee survey or market research questionnaire might be far more revealing than just having them tick boxes or similar. You might find that previously hidden insights are revealed.

Phrase open questions so respondents tell you what they are really thinking, and just ask for a few lines of feedback to make your question quick to answer.

TRAINING

Stories help participants connect emotionally to the storyteller (trainer) and to the 'lesson'. That emotional attachment helps create the buy-in and facilitate learning transfer.

Try to think of a short story that can help embed each learning point.

Also, asking participants for their experiences (stories) of good and bad practice of your training topic, what they learnt from their experience and how they can apply that lesson in business, might be more effective than running through a standard 'off-the-shelf' course.

'HOW TO' MANUALS

As mentioned in an earlier chapter, when Xerox recognised that its repair staff learned to repair machines by sharing stories rather than by reading 'how to' manuals, they established the now extremely valuable Eureka database.

Your company, like all others, probably has 'how to' manuals on topics ranging from health and safety to how to use the company intranet. If any of these 'how to' manuals are 'owned' by your team or department, could you build your own 'Eureka' database to replace these manuals?

TEAM BUILDING & COACHING

Stories that show how other teams have successfully handled conflict, overcome obstacles and surpassed goals can help show how your team can do the same.

You could try a round-robin style sharing of personal stories at an appropriate team event. It might help foster a greater team spirit. And are the stories your team currently share as empowering as they could be?

Coaching

Coaching is an essential management activity if we are to get the best from those who work for us. At times it can be useful to share stories that allow the coachee to see beyond the immediate issue, and at other times it is helpful to spot the stories your coachee tells about themselves.

Often their stories are based on a value-based interpretation rather than being supported by hard facts, and all too frequently set self-imposed limits.

WHERE TO USE STORIES

EXERCISE

Think about the proactive steps you can take today to help your team, department or company adopt storytelling.

Can you build a few storytelling minutes into your regular team meetings?

Perhaps share stories of your experiences in the previous period and how they have helped team goals?

Could you organise lunchtime storytelling sessions that focus on specific topics like innovation or customers. These sessions might be a rich source of untapped knowledge that could be put to practical use.

STORYTELLING RESOURCES

INTRODUCTION

To help you advance your storytelling skills, in this chapter I will:

- Set out some of the personal story-lines I use in day-to-day business to get various messages across

- Provide you with a list of books where you can obtain 'other people's stories'

- Share with you some story quotes, as they can help to encourage people to use storytelling

- Finally, give you a 4-week plan you can follow to help you enhance your skills and find your own personal storytelling style

STORYTELLING RESOURCES

PERSONAL STORY-LINES

Here are a few of my personal story-lines to help spark some ideas.

Oh no!: I went on a rock climbing course when I was 23 years old. I was as fit as my fellow aspiring rock climbers, but I kept saying to myself 'oh no! this is really difficult' – consequently I didn't become a very good climber.

Message – the words you say to yourself dictate what you accomplish.

PERSONAL STORY-LINES

Thunder-guts: Nickname of the school maths teacher. The school set career expectation that boys should get apprenticeships in the local dockyard. Thunder-guts challenged this expectation and inspired me to go to university.

Message – set high expectations and you are likely to reach them.

Negotiating at customs: In 1984 I was travelling in Africa on a tight budget. At Kinshasa airport, reluctant to pay the customary $25 bribe to officials, I gave them instead four 'golden delicious' apples. The officials were very happy with these.

Message – it is possible to change the rules of negotiation and think what the other side really wants.

PERSONAL STORY-LINES

Hitchhiking policeman: In 1985, in Malawi, I was travelling on my own in a hire car. There were endless police road-blocks. A policeman stopped me, to check my documents I assumed. Instead, to my surprise, he jumped into the passenger seat clasping a bunch of bananas, and asked for a lift to the capital, Lilongwe, where he was going on a course. He directed me via an off-the-beaten-track route, where I met his relatives and saw places tourists don't go to.
Message – embrace serendipity.

Brown envelope: In 1986 the oil price was plummeting and I was made redundant as an oil exploration geologist. Wondering what to do next, a chance conversation with an older friend encouraged me to embrace change and so I decided to take an MBA degree.
Message – change can happen at anytime – embrace it.

95

PERSONAL STORY-LINES

Father's eulogy: My father died after a long illness. Writing and delivering his eulogy made me reflect on my own ambitions.
Message – focus on what you want to do.

New York marathon: In 1999, though unfit, I trained for the NY marathon. During training I was told to make changes to my diet and my running style. On the day I hit 'the wall' at mile 21. Failure loomed. But I changed my running style and managed to complete the marathon.
Message – make changes to achieve your goal.

Wise words: In 2002 I had an executive coaching assignment with the Chairman of a large, well-known firm. He was a very experienced man, a few years from retirement and highly regarded by his industry peers. When I asked why he wanted coaching, he said, *'If I learn one thing from our work together, the investment will have been worthwhile'*.
Message – be a life learner.

PERSONAL STORY-LINES

Stand-up comedy: In 2008 I realised that I needed to practise what I often preached, and move out of my own comfort zone. I'd always wanted to try stand-up comedy but had been too nervous to try it in front of an audience. I set myself a goal to do a gig and actually performed a 10 minute stint at a comedy club in London, with some of my clients in the audience.

Message – constantly stretch yourself to achieve your goals.

OTHER PEOPLE'S STORIES

If you take a look at the business bestseller lists in any of the online bookstores, you will probably find that many of the titles listed contain stories that could suit your storytelling goals. Biographies, history books and stories of inventions can also be great sources of other people's stories. Here are a few books you might find of interest:

Beyer R, *The Greatest Stories Never Told: 100 Tales From History To Astonish, Bewilder, and Stupefy*
Harper (2003)

Cialdini R.B, *Influence: The Psychology of Persuasion*
Harper Collins (2006)

DeLong T. J, *Flying Without a Net*
Harvard Business Review Press (2011)

Gladwell M, *David & Goliath*
Penguin Group (2013)

OTHER PEOPLE'S STORIES CONT'D

Heath Chip & Dan, *Decisive: How to make better choices in life and work*
Random House Publishing (2013)

Kahneman D, *Thinking, Fast and Slow*
Penguin Group (2011)

Panati C, *Extraordinary Origins of Everyday Things*
Harper Perennial (1989)

Peters Dr S, *The Chimp Paradox*
Vermilion (2012)

Robinson K and Aronica L, *The Element: How Finding your Passion Changes Everything*
Penguin (2009)

Shirky C, *Here Comes Everybody: How Change Happens When People Come Together*
Penguin (2009)

STORY QUOTES

Including story quotes in your presentations or written communications, where appropriate, can be a great way to start sowing the benefits of storytelling. Here are a few quotes you might find useful:

The principal vehicle of leadership is the story: the leader affects individual behaviour, thought, and feelings through the stories that he or she tells.

Professor Howard Gardner, Harvard University

The stories that people tell are the container that holds their world together and gives meaning to their lives.

Andrew Ramer

STORY QUOTES

There is no substitute for the story told out loud...for the living gesture that interprets human understanding.

D. M. Dooling

Human beings are a story; they are living a story and anyone open to this story is living a huge part – perhaps all – of themselves.

P. L. Travers

The storyteller takes what he tells from experience – his own or that reported by others – and he in turn makes it the experience of those who are listening to his tale.

Walter Benjamin

Storytelling reveals meaning without committing the error of defining it.

Hannah Arendt

STORY QUOTES

> *Tell your tales;*
> *make them true.*
> *If they endure,*
> *so will you.*

James Keller

> *Storytelling is where we share*
> *what we've discovered; all of*
> *us have discovered a little*
> *secret about life.*

Michael Cotter

> *Storytelling is the*
> *most powerful way*
> *to put ideas into the*
> *world today.*

Robert McKee

STORY QUOTES

As I'm telling stories about my life I'm holding up a mirror to my listeners, trying to jog their memories, getting them to look at their stories, the tales that lace their lives.

Elizabeth Ellis

As the Inuit asks the visitor coming in out of the cold; speak so that I may see you.

David Rothenberg

Draw your chair up close to the precipice and I'll tell you a story.

F. Scott Fitzgerald

YOUR 4-WEEK PLAN

 WEEK ONE

Once you have completed the exercises and reflected on the questions posed in previous chapters, follow this four week plan. It will help you hone your skills and find a storytelling style you feel comfortable with.

- Think of your objective for wanting to become a great storyteller

- Note down one thing you can do this week to ensure you embed or 'perform' this outcome

- Add to your personal story library so you have five stories in total

- Tell a story in a business setting (ie presentation, meeting or coaching)

- Identify a story you hear in your organisation that demonstrates its values

YOUR 4-WEEK PLAN

WEEK TWO

- Watch a film and observe how the characters and plot are developed

- Be a story detective and browse the national papers, trade journals, books, or watch TV, and note another three stories that resonate with you

- Tell a story in a business setting (ie presentation, meeting or coaching session)

- Ask someone to give you feedback on a story you have told (what was the point of your story and how did they interpret the point of it? What did they infer about you from the story you told?)

- Identify at least two stories your customers tell others about your organisation's products or services

YOUR 4-WEEK PLAN

- Continue to add to your personal story list; aim to have at least 10 by the end of this week

- Think of the meaning of each story

- Look at each story on your list and note down the situations where you can use it

- Encourage someone who works for or with you to tell you the 'story' behind the facts or process they have told you? Did this allow you to learn something new?

- Can you, this week, identify any stories your executives tell to inspire staff?

STORYTELLING RESOURCES

YOUR 4-WEEK PLAN

WEEK FOUR

- Continue to add to your personal story list, so you now have 20 personal stories in total

- Think of the meaning of each story

- Look through your list – do you see any 'signature' stories leaping out

- Note down three stories you hear about your organisation when you are at work

- Aim to tell three different stories this week in business settings

- Think of a presentation you deliver often or an upcoming one: how can you add stories into it to make it more persuasive, engaging and/or inspiring?

IN CONCLUSION

In 1996 at the conference in Mexico, my heart sank as I recognized what a poor job I had done, as a leader, in trying to inspire my audience with my logic, rather than with stories. It was then that I realised that storytelling solves the problem I had faced in the past – how to get your message to 'stick' and inspire people to take action.

If you follow the easy steps in this pocketbook (think of the types of stories you can tell; develop your own story library; develop your stories; tell them effectively; use them when appropriate in day-to-day business) and follow the 4-week plan, then you too very soon will be like the CEO I watched at the conference in Mexico and will deliver a great talk based around stories. And, who knows, you may just receive a standing ovation.

As you practise your storytelling skills, be prepared to refine your stories so they resonate and work well with your various audiences. Some at first may work better than others. And recall the story I told about my days of learning Spanish, and do the opposite. Aim to practise your storytelling skills in business **every day**.

IN CONCLUSION

All great leaders are invariably great storytellers. Tell pragmatic stories and show your team, colleagues and boss that you are a great leader.

Pocketbooks – *available in both paperback and digital formats*

360 Degree Feedback*
Absence Management
Appraisals
Assertiveness
Balance Sheet
Body Language
Business Planning
Career Transition
Coaching
Cognitive Behavioural Coaching
Communicator's
Competencies
Confidence
Creative Manager's
C.R.M.
Cross-cultural Business
Customer Service
Decision-making
Delegation
Developing People
Discipline & Grievance
Diversity*
Emotional Intelligence
Empowerment*
Energy and Well-being
Facilitator's
Feedback
Flexible Working*

Handling Complaints
Handling Resistance
Icebreakers
Impact & Presence
Improving Efficiency
Improving Profitability
Induction
Influencing
Interviewer's
I.T. Trainer's
Key Account Manager's
Leadership
Learner's
Management Models
Manager's
Managing Assessment Centres
Managing Budgets
Managing Cashflow
Managing Change
Managing Customer Service
Managing Difficult Participants
Managing Recruitment
Managing Upwards
Managing Your Appraisal
Marketing
Meetings
Memory
Mentoring

Motivation
Negotiator's
Networking
NLP
Nurturing Innovation
Openers & Closers
People Manager's
Performance Management
Personal Success
Positive Mental Attitude
Presentations
Problem Behaviour
Project Management
Psychometric Testing
Resolving Conflict
Reward
Sales Excellence
Salesperson's*
Self-managed Development
Starting In Management
Storytelling
Strategy
Stress
Succeeding at Interviews
Sustainability
Tackling Difficult Conversations
Talent Management
Teambuilding Activities

Teamworking
Telephone Skills
Telesales*
Thinker's
Time Management
Trainer's
Training Evaluation
Training Needs Analysis
Transfer of Learning
Virtual Teams
Vocal Skills
Working Relationships
Workplace Politics
Writing Skills

* only available as an e-book

Pocketfiles

Trainer's Blue Pocketfile of
Ready-to-use Activities

Trainer's Green Pocketfile of
Ready-to-use Activities

Trainer's Red Pocketfile of
Ready-to-use Activities

To order please visit us at **www.pocketbook.co.uk**

About the Author

Roger E. Jones
Roger is the coach & advisor to CEOs, executive team members and top teams committed to achieving their full potential. A best-selling international author, he has conducted business in over 40 countries.

Working collaboratively with clients worldwide, Roger helps leaders tackle the most important organisational challenges, including performance transformation, behavioural change and senior team effectiveness.

He is an engaging and insightful keynote conference speaker and his work has been featured by the *BBC, Forbes, The Sunday Times* and the *Financial Times*. In addition to *The Storytelling Pocketbook*, his other books include: *Key Account Manager's Pocketbook* and *What Can Chief Executives Learn From Stand-Up Comedians?*

In addition to an MBA (Cranfield) and MSc & BSc (Hons) degrees, he is studying for an Executive Masters Degree at INSEAD in Consulting and Coaching for Change (completion 2014). It integrates a range of psychological disciplines and goes deep into the drivers of leadership behaviours and the hidden dynamics of teams and organisations.

To book Roger to speak at your next company or industry conference, or to discover more about how he can assist your leaders and top teams, please visit www.RogerEdwardJones.com or contact him on telephone 44 (0)20 8878 3429 or email roger@rogeredwardjones.com

Your details

Name _____

Position _____

Company _____

Address _____

_____

_____

Telephone _____

Fax _____

E-mail _____

VAT No. (EC companies) _____

Your Order Ref _____

LRC
NEW COLLEGE
SWINDON

Please send me:

		No. copies
The Storytelling	Pocketbook	☐
The _____	Pocketbook	☐
The _____	Pocketbook	☐
The _____	Pocketbook	☐

Order by Post

MANAGEMENT POCKETBOOKS LTD

LAUREL HOUSE, STATION APPROACH,
ALRESFORD, HAMPSHIRE SO24 9JH UK

Order by Phone, Fax or Internet
Telephone: +44 (0)1962 735573
Facsimile: +44 (0)1962 733637
Email: sales@pocketbook.co.uk
Web: www.pocketbook.co.uk

Customers in USA should contact:
Management Pocketbooks
2427 Bond Street, University Park, IL 60466
Telephone: 866 620 6944   Facsimile: 708 534 7803
Email: mp.orders@ware-pak.com
Web: www.managementpocketbooks.com